THE SMALL BUSINESS
OWNER'S MANUAL

THE SMALL BUSINESS OWNER'S MANUAL

Build Your Dream Business

Jerry Isenhour
Ed Krow
Patricia Lawrence

ISBN: 1979246599
ISBN 13: 9781979246590
Library of Congress Control Number: 2017917136
CreateSpace Independent Publishing Platform
North Charleston, South Carolina

INTRODUCTION

S o, you want to start a business, be an entrepreneur, and build a machine to take you to your dreams? Congratulations—this is what America is all about. But here are the facts: most small businesses fail. The statistics are alarming. But the reason they fail is obvious and common. Michael Gerber, in the *E-Myth*, says most businesspeople fail when they start a business because they are technicians and have an entrepreneurial seizure. As the reality sinks in, they start to sink. Many times, one's life savings can be lost, and the financial destruction can be massive.

The purpose of this book is to share with you what we call a GPS—a compass to guide you to the business you want to have. This book was written after working with hundreds of businesses over the years and noting the problems and issues that they had in common.

The research for this book has been underway for several years. During this time, we analyzed a number of small businesses via an inside look that very few are privy to. The result of this research was the finding that the main difference between businesses that failed and those that succeeded was having a system. And once the system is properly designed and executed, success of the business becomes much more likely.

It is the opinion of the authors that a person entering the realm of entrepreneurship would be well served to be a well-read individual and study the words of experts who can assist him or her in moving to the desire level. The following is a list of books that we suggest a person should read and review before entering the business world. And if you find you do not have the time or patience to do this, then it is advised that you *stop* and not move forward, because success will be very hard, perhaps impossible, to ever attain.

The E Myth, by Michael Gerber
In his book, Mr. Gerber details how many are caught up in the excitement of the prospect of self-employment and how they enter this with what he refers to as an entrepreneurial seizure. They have a great idea, and they jump in head first. In the process, they often become lost and, in the ensuing years, find themselves, if they are lucky, floundering, and the dreams remain well out of their reach. In a worst-case scenario, they find themselves out of business and perhaps in the worst debt they have ever imagined, with savings and even homes (that they used for collateral) gone—perhaps even bankrupt.

Traction, by Gino Wickman
In *Traction*, Mr. Wickman talks of the entrepreneurial operating system (EOS), which is a method by which management can put together plans to reach their dreams. Mr. Wickman talks about accountability and the benefit of short-term goals, what he refers to as "ROCKS." Combined with *The E Myth*, these two works, in the opinion of the authors, should be viewed as the bible for the small-business owner.

Failing Forward, by Dr. John Maxwell
You must become a leader, and as a leader, you must learn that in life there will be failures. In fact, the person who cannot learn from his or her failings is destined to never achieve greatness. You see, we often dread failure. We often will not step outside of our comfort zone due to our fear of failure, though failure is a part of life, and in fact we should celebrate our failures as they give us the strength to move forward. Often, failure is just the prescription many of us need to build the better mousetrap we know the world needs and that we can provide.

21 Laws of Leadership, by Dr. John Maxwell
As the owner of a business, one of the skills required, no matter the size of the business, is leadership. Leadership is required for you to properly lead others, and the

people you lead will be varied. In this book, Dr. Maxwell has detailed the twenty-one irrefutable laws that every leader must strive to master. As you read this, you will find (if you are honest with yourself) that you have already conquered and possess some of them, but others you have not. As a leader, your aim should be to make your strengths better and make your weaknesses into strengths.

IS A COLLEGE DEGREE REQUIRED?

Here is the opinion of the authors: a college degree may well be a help to you. Let's face it; all learning has value. But is a college degree required for success? We would have to say no, it is not. In fact, many with college degrees will attest that the skills they have learned in real life far outweigh the formal education they received.

Now, do not take this as an attack on a formal education, as all education is beneficial, but many people without a college degree have been successful in life and have grown astounding business models. So the point here is, is a college degree good? Of course it is. Is it required? No, it is not. But to move forward as a business owner, you must now commit yourself to continuous education to move to the level you aspire to.

1

SO ARE YOU READY TO START?

G reat! There is only one place to start, and that is at the beginning. And so, this is how we begin: with the steps required to take the business you dream of and make it one where reality meets and even exceeds the dream you hold so dear.

Now, as we move forward, have you done the recommended reading? You see, a person approaching something such as building a business requires knowledge, and this knowledge is gained by reading the words of great business minds. The books on the recommended reading list were suggested because they are all great analytical works and can greatly contribute to your level of success. The nonapplication of these principles could well be the reason for your failure.

Let's roll up our sleeves and make it happen now!

2

WHAT IS YOUR PRODUCT OR SERVICE?

Is your idea a product? Is it a service? Is it a combination of the two? So you think you have got a better mousetrap or have a widget that no one has ever built before? Perhaps you have a service: Is it new, or is it a better one? Or have you invented a new process that will bring a product to the market at a lower cost? Maybe you have even developed a great idea that people will buy: ideas are valuable, so don't think that is a crazy thought at all.

Going forward, "product" refers to a service, object, process, or idea that you feel has value and that others will buy. This is commerce, and commerce is how a business runs.

So as you begin your foray into the world of your own business, you must first identify the product:

What is it?
Why will it sell?
Why will it be profitable?

This may well be a critical decision point, because you must have a decision on this to move forward. Without a profitable product, you are doomed to failure.

Now, a part of this decision making and accumulation of the needed data will involve research. You cannot simply make the decision based on what you think: after all, no matter how great the product is, the market must also agree; otherwise, how will it ever sell (and no matter other factors, sales are a crucial issue)?

You may want to use the system that larger companies use when they launch products: they use focus groups. We will talk about focus groups later in this book. The focus group, drawn from different segments of the market you plan to penetrate, can provide you valuable input that is better learned in the focus setting than with products that are sitting on a shelf rotting due to no demand. There are millions of those— make sure yours is not one of them. An ironclad rule for success is that the product must sell!

Or have you considered bypassing the product or service concept-development process altogether in favor of buying into a franchise? While this may sound like a shorter path to achieving your entrepreneurial ambitions, there are still plenty of considerations that you must weigh, such as the following:

1) How much money do you need to ensure success? Aside from the franchise fee, how much working capital will you need until your franchise starts turning a profit? How long does it typically take to achieve breakeven?
2) How much money will your business pay you? This is an extremely important answer to have up front.
3) What does the franchise investment cover? Again, it is critical to know how long it will take for your franchise to reach breakeven, so you understand how much cash you need and how long it will last.

Either direction you take, you'll need to feel confident in your product.

3

WHAT IS YOUR MARKET?

So who is your market? Who do you foresee will buy the product?

In this step, you must define the market and determine why consumers will buy your product. What makes your product the one the market is looking for? Or if they are not looking for it, how will your market accept your product? Let's face it—selling air conditioners is much easier in Florida than it is in Alaska, isn't it?

So let's answer the question—just who are your customers? And along with that, why will your product appeal to them? You must remember that market appeal consists of many things: a part is the presentation, and another is the role the product plays in the customer's life.

You see, you may think you have the greatest product in the world, but if your customers don't agree, will it sell? Not likely, unless you use an extremely strong enticement to buy it. However, there are millions of these products in your customers' lives, and the problem is they do not get used, they provide no value, and they certainly do not build sales.

Look around your own home, your office, or in your life. How many products have you bought that went into a drawer, a cabinet, or the trash can? Examine your market: Who will buy, will they use it, and will they recommend it to their friends?

4

DO A MARKET ANALYSIS—WILL THE MARKET SUPPORT YOUR BUSINESS VENTURE?

This is such a tough area, and one where a crystal ball would provide phenomenal assistance. But the problem is we rarely have a crystal ball at our disposal—and so few of us would even know how to use it if we did.

But this is where, if you survey your market, you can accumulate the data that you need to make an educated decision.

The greatest business, product, or service in the world (and there are millions of them) will die if there is not a market demand. And if you are introducing a new product never seen before, the questions you must answer are these: How will you build this market, why do people want it, and why will they buy it?

All of this takes deep deliberation; we may even call this soul-searching. This must be approached from an unemotional position. Business decisions based on emotion often are later called bad decisions.

There are new methods of data collection that can give you a lot of useful information that can be reviewed as you are putting together your plan for this great new enterprise you are assembling. This I refer to as doing your homework.

So do some research. It is a lot easier to start with the right idea than to learn later that no one else agrees with the great idea you had. And if your target market doesn't agree, then likely your product won't sell.

You should consider: Are you selling a product in a market where you will be competing with what others are already offering? If so, what is it that makes yours so special? This is a hard question. Of course, you may well realize the benefits of what you offer, but the question is, will the market recognize it?

If your product is something new, not available before in your market, what will drive the demand for the product? While we would like to think that everyone will want what we have to offer, it is still best to run these thoughts through your analysis process now. It is much easier to conquer these issues prior to beginning and much less costly than building something that cannot be sold. There is nothing worse that offering a product or service that the customer does not share your enthusiasm for.

5

COMPETITION—ARE YOU BUILDING A NEW MOUSETRAP OR A BETTER MOUSETRAP?

Who is your competition for the customer? Often, your competition is as close as the mirror, as each business owner must realize that in the pursuit of success, your number-one competitor will always be you. But we must delve deeper. As a new enterprise, you must strategize thoroughly how you will enter the market and how your product will surpass the competition.

So first, to borrow a commonly used term of the past, let's talk about your product as a mousetrap.

Do you plan to build a better mousetrap, or will it just be another one like all the others? If the market is underserved, what will bring the mousetrap buyers to you? You can make big inroads in a market, but the most successful do this through what is called disruption of the market. As you examine the marketplace, you will find many who have done this successfully. An example of this is Uber. They saw a way to disrupt the transportation market by using people with cars and put together a marketing program that has taken a percentage of the market. Now we see Lyft as setting up to go after that market as well. But what Uber did was unique, and it was so popular that in certain airports, taxi companies were successful in preventing them from picking up. One example is Los Angeles International Airport, LAX—Uber can take you there but can't pick you up. Now examine Lyft. What is their market positioning doing to take their share of the transportation market?

Another example is Dollar Shave Club. They took a product that was commonly available and turned it into an overnight success. And they continue to grow this market successfully by using various forms of social marketing. They succeeded by developing a new way to deliver the product to the customer. It made sense, and they have built a significant share of the razor-blade market. But once you develop a market, be aware someone else may want a share of it. An example of this is that now Harry's Shave wants a piece of the same market. How will they do it? Lower prices, better service, or higher quality? This is an example of market disruption where a new way of delivering product can take it to new heights. No less can be said about the success of Amazon over longtime retailers such as Sears. Again, the secret for this was not so much the products themselves but rather the way the products were bought and delivered.

The same thought process exists if you are building a new product. Again, it goes back to these questions: How will the market accept it, and how are you destined to have a successful product and not one simply sitting on shelves?

There are two schools of thought. Let's apply our thought processes to Dollar Shave Club and Uber. Each of them duplicated a product or service that was commonly available. They broke the mold by disrupting the market—they came at it from a new aspect, a new method of delivery of the product. There were plenty of ways to obtain shaving products before Dollar Shave Club; what they did was change the way we buy. They sold convenience.

The same is true of Uber. They changed the way the product was purchased, and they changed the way a business was operated. Unlike a normal taxi or car service, they simply went to market with the cars that their drivers owned. What they took to market was a new method of transportation that users love and that traditional taxi companies hate.

6

ROAD MAP TO THE FUTURE / OUTLINE OF HOW YOU WILL BUILD YOUR BUSINESS AND HOW YOU WILL EXIT IT

But before you go further, let's examine a critical question. What is your planned exit from this business? Is this a business you plan to build and sell, or is this a business you plan to be in for many years?

One of the secrets to building a business of value is to build it to sell, even though you may never plan to sell it. Often, we decide at a later point we need to do something different, that the business we built is not the right match for our life's work. There is no greater feeling of entrapment than to have a business you have poured you time, blood, and tears into (not to mention your funds) and then learn it has no value to a buyer.

Often, entrepreneurs will decide that they want to divest themselves of their business, and it is at this stage that they find that the business they have invested their time and their hard-earned dollars, and even shed tears over, now holds no value. This is all too often the case in small-business America. Think back over your own lifetime. Do you remember businesses that at one time were around you and that one day they simply disappeared? Or watch for a "going out of business" sale—that is, someone selling business assets because the business itself no longer has value in the market. Or the worst is the company you see being auctioned off, piece by piece. That is often an auction of someone's life.

Therefore, decide from the beginning what is your plan for getting out. And from day one, build your business so that the value will be there when the day comes you decide to divest yourself of it. If you plan to give to a son or a daughter, then give them value, not a big box of problems that they hate, or they do not want.

And this is also a point to consider. Many small-business owners build a business, and their plan is that this will be a legacy. The problem is that the ones they depend on to carry the legacy simply do not want it.

Hence, this must be a part of your business plan: building a business that has value. And that is best done with the thought that you plan to sell it; then, no matter the results, it will have value.

7

WHAT ARE THE POTENTIAL ROADBLOCKS TO SUCCESS OF THE VENTURE?

This is like mapping a trip. You know what it feels like to be headed down an interstate, going at a good clip, and suddenly up ahead you see brake lights, and the traffic is starting to slow down and stop. And you think to yourself, "If I had just had my GPS on, I would have known this was happening and could have changed course and headed around it."

Now let's be clear; no one can predict the future. But we can take steps to predict the potential roadblocks to our business. And every business and every product will face roadblocks.

As such, you need to face this going in. Is your product one that will be bought using discretionary money? If so, it is likely that people will no longer buy it when their discretionary income drops. Is your product weather dependent? Many have faced financial ruin when the weather one year did not provide the impetus for customers to buy. There are a multitude of reasons; however, the questions that must be answered are these: What are the potential roadblocks we will face, and how can we navigate a course around them?

It will most likely require that you add new skills. You see, as you build a business, you also must build your skills as a leader. As John Maxwell says in his book *The 21 Irrefutable Laws of Leadership*, anyone can steer the ship, but few can chart the course. The thought you must put to the forefront of your mind is that you are now going to be charting the course. And the course you select will likely affect the health and welfare of your business, yourself, and those who will depend on your business and your product.

8

WHAT IS YOUR ROLE IN THE VENTURE / WHAT ARE YOUR START POSITION AND GOAL POSITION / WHAT IS YOUR SELF-EXAMINATION OF SKILLS?

What are you good at? What do you suck at? What are your skills? What skills do you not possess? Can you build the skills you do not possess?

Running a successful business requires a lot of hats, and many times we fail to recognize that we cannot wear all the hats at the same time. This should not be taken as a reason not to move forward but rather a realization of the fact that if we apply these principles in our start-up process and thinking, it will alleviate future problems very well.

One of the best resources is the (previously recommended) book *Traction*. It explains the need for two personalities in the successful business-building model. *Traction* calls them the visionary and the integrator (the authors of this book prefer the term *implementer*). The skills of the visionary and the skills of the integrator are those required at the top, but both skills are not necessarily found in the mind of the same person.

The visionary is the person who has the vision; he can paint the most beautiful picture possible of that dream's destination. He can see it and, in a way, almost taste, touch, and smell it. It is there; it is a living, breathing dream. But the visionary is often halted at the stage of action, better called implementation.

It also takes the skills of the integrator, or as the authors prefer, the implementer. She is the person who can see and hear the beautiful picture the visionary presents, but her skills are turning this vision into reality. This is likely the person who makes it happen.

But there are lots of hats in the business that must be worn, and each must be worn in such a manner that excellence and commitment are a part of the description of the person. In the later portions of this book, we will address in much more depth the various hats that must be worn for success.

Now, as you start the business, you will be faced with a cold fact: you either must pay someone to wear some of the hats, or you will need to wear all the hats. This will be discussed in depth in the chapter on accountability charts.

But for now, do the self-examination and decide what your role will be from start-up through exit—it is all a part of the plan. You must also remember that a plan is never written in stone. As the business matures, likely your business plan will also be modified to meet the changing needs of the business, and likely your role as the owner will change too. Therefore, periodic review and modification are required for any successful venture!

9

INITIAL FUNDING OF BUSINESS FOR START-UP

Here is a cold, hard fact: it takes money to start a business. A major failing of too many great businesses is the lack of money to properly fund the business operation. *Funding* is the word commonly used in business discussions when we speak of this fact.

So it is time to sit down and look at just how much money it will take. Most will underestimate this cost because there likely will be unexpected business expenses that will arise. Read on to the next chapter as we discuss these funding needs.

Not all funding money is created equal. That is in effect saying, when you start looking for funds for your business, you'll need to know what strings are attached. If it is your own money, no worries—you make the rules for that pot of cash. However, if you are considering using other people's money (OPM) to fund your business, you'll need to stop and ask yourself these tough questions:

- Are you willing to go into debt and repay over time?
- Are you willing to give up some amount of equity/ownership in your company?
- Are you willing to put your personal assets at risk to guarantee a loan?
- How much control over the company are you willing to give up to an equity partner?
- Do you need other assistance from a funder besides just money?
- How big do you want to grow?
- How fast do you want to grow?
- What relationship (if any) do you want to have with a funder?

Whatever route you choose, you need to be objective and take any emotion out of this part of the transaction. This situation needs to be handled in a business-like manner with everything *in writing*, even if you are borrowing from family. Remember, some of the ugliest family feuds come about because of money. Don't let this happen to you.

Your fledgling business can also be a source of funding. You sell to your customers, they pay you, and you reinvest the profits in growing your business. This is by far the best way to grow—sometimes called bootstrapping—especially if you're going to demonstrate to banks and other funding sources the validity and sustainability of your business model. On the other hand, it can also be a slower and more controlled path to growing your business.

The way you choose to fund your business needs to be *your* decision. You must be comfortable with what you will or won't put at risk, the amount you borrow, the conditions you accept, how fast you grow, and so forth. It may not seem like it, but you are the one in control of this decision.

TAKING ON DEBT
Funding with debt will give you the advantage of retaining control over your business, but you'll have to play by the bank's rules and qualify based on the bank's criteria. If you have good credit, not too much personal debt, and some paid-off assets, you could be a good candidate for traditional bank or credit union funding.

So how does the bank decide you're worth the risk? The loan officer has a lot of fancy phrases for the factors she considers (debt-to-asset ratio, for one), but basically, she'll look at your business's total assets, your ability to generate enough money to pay back your loan, and how much risk you're willing to share with the bank.

WHAT YOU'RE WORTH
The loan officer looks first at your business's total assets. For example, that would include any money in the business's bank accounts, the workshop and office you own, and the two trucks you already have.

HOW MUCH MONEY CAN YOU MAKE?

A loan officer will then examine deeply your business's ability to generate enough money to cover your loan payments. He calls this the "debt service coverage ratio" (but remember, he likes these kinds of phrases).

WHAT'S YOUR SKIN IN THE GAME?

Our loan officer is now ready to look at how much you're willing to put on the line to make your loan happen. He calls this the loan-to-value, or LTV, ratio. In English, this means that he divides your loan amount by the price of what you're looking to buy.

FUNDING WITH EQUITY

Unlike debt, equity allows you to avoid the personal risk that comes with loan guarantees. An equity investor makes an investment in the business for a return that is to be generated by future profits. A portion of these profits will go to the investor, who has taken shares or a percentage of ownership in your company. If the company never makes money, the investor will never be repaid. In simple terms, you have gained a partner. To mitigate the risk of not recouping his or her investment, the equity investor may request a role in certain decision-making aspects of the business.

Equity is a common way to fund a start-up business. In the tech world, venture capital investors and angel investors pump millions of dollars into start-ups each year—some never see these start-ups generate their first dollar of revenue. However, some make it big and then go public—Google, Facebook, and the like—delivering huge returns to their initial investors. But then, not everyone is a Google or Facebook start-up and must make the real decision around how to fund their start-up activities.

In addition to deciding on debt or equity, you'll need to consider the following factors when selecting one or more funding sources:

- Will your funding sources stand by you in good and not-so-good times?
- Do your funding sources act objectively and professionally?
- Do they maintain open communications with you?

- Do they have a high degree of integrity and honesty?
- Do they value your skills and abilities?

Remember, the way you choose to fund your business needs to be *your* decision.

10

FUNDING / BUDGET / FINANCES / ANTICIPATED RETURN

Well, here we are: maybe you will love this section, maybe you will hate it, or maybe you will endure it. But the all-important factor that we must look at is the funding requirements for the business.

So have you reviewed this? You need to consider not only the start-up costs but also the operating costs and the ongoing business expenses. There will be overhead expenses—every month. What are the fixed expenses of the business going to be? They must be accurately estimated.

If you want an idea of the type of funding required, another place to research is the Internet. The research vehicle will be a search for the cost for franchises. Now this is not to send you out to buy a franchise, even though that may be a direction you decide you need to go. If you research franchises, you will find they list three funding requirements. One is the buy in; this usually is the cost you are paying for their proprietary intellectual property. Now, as you look at these, you may find these are high costs. But keep in mind that what they are sharing with you is the result of a lot of hard work, a lot of mistakes, and perhaps how they were ultimately successful. Buying a franchise may not be a good fit for a lot of people, because the franchise is presenting you with both a plan and the ways to make it happen.

Next, the franchise will tell you the start-up costs. These will cover the cost of the start-up of the business. And lastly, they will detail the operating funds the business will need once the doors are open.

Now, this research will help you, as it is an eye-opening experience to start to look at the funding that may be required for your business. There are a multitude of business models and a multitude of different cost factors.

Thus, what you must do is put together these anticipated costs, and the way this is done is through what we call the budget, one of the most important parts of your GPS.

The budget is a quantifying tool. It forecasts the income, it forecasts the expenses, and it forecasts the cash flow. It also considers the needs of the business for expansion or other changes and asks the hard question: that is a great idea, but where is the money going to come from? This is often a moment of truth when a business owner sits and faces that great resource, one who may feel like an adversary but is not. This is the chief financial officer (or CFO).

A budget will allow you to estimate the amount of initial funding you will need for your start-up. When most folks hear the word budget, they think of how much they will sell for the year. However, to get a full picture of your company and its performance, we recommend budgeting for your income statement (a.k.a. profit and loss, or P&L) and cash flow statement, at a minimum. This will give you a clearer picture of the cash requirements and profitability of your business, as well as provide your GPS with the data to guide you through the financial management of your company for the year. You see, your GPS lays out the path to achieve your business goals, in monthly increments. If the goals of each month are achieved individually, then the year and long-term goals will be achieved!

To get you started building your GPS for the year, here are the items that you will need to consider and quantify for your P&L:

- Revenue target
- Seasonality of your revenue (slower/higher sales periods)
- Marketing plans and their cost
- Facilities expense

- Cost of your product or service
- Labor cost to produce or deliver your product/service
- Selling expenses
- Supplier and distribution expenses
- Equipment required (one-time expenditures and ongoing replacements)
- Research and development for product improvements
- Technology
- Operational costs
- Insurances
- Administrative costs
- Compensation and benefits
- Staffing requirements and hiring expenses
- Professional services
- Start-up expenses (prerevenue)

In addition to the items above for the P&L, you will also need to budget for your cash flow requirements. This will require knowing or estimating:

- Debt service requirements (paying off your loan)
- Payment terms for your customers (will you be paid in ninety days or fifteen days for what you sell?)
- Payment terms to your vendors (will you pay them in ninety days or fifteen days for what you buy from them?)
- Owner's draw (paid to owner in lieu of salary in sole proprietorships and partnerships)
- Owner's distribution (paid to owner to cover taxes and other items)
- Purchases of property
- Business acquisition/divestiture

11

ACCOUNTABILITY CHART / ORGANIZATIONAL CHART

Accountability and organization charts: this is the time to build them. Do not think that they are for a later time, after the business has matured. Again, this is a part of the process that will require periodic review and modification. The GPS may have to be tweaked for any number of reasons; a business must be amenable to required changes due to any factors that can affect its success. A common failing of many businesses is the failure to perform this periodic review. In reviewing the history of American businesses, you will find that many businesses that did not modify and reinvent themselves as required have either disappeared or are disappearing, as we read in the news almost daily. It would be good to reflect on your own memories: What businesses were strong ten or twenty years ago and have disappeared or are failing now?

As business strategists and consultants, we see this as a major area of concern that many do not deal with in the beginning. New business owners often believe they must do everything, but organizational charts are a much-needed part of the formula to build a successful enterprise.

To run a business, it will require wearing many different hats. Yes, at the beginning most entrepreneurs assume these hats; some they are good at, and others perhaps are not within their skill set. And there must be the self-awareness that some are simply beyond our present skill levels. As such, one must endeavor to learn these skills or hire or contract for them. Even though many wear all the hats in the beginning, it is also important to establish a process that, as the business grows, we already know what hats we will remove and place upon another person's head. Provided below is a list of the typical job roles or positions in an average business. Some of these may not be found in the business you are building; just delete them from your list.

Two books that we have suggested will present a lot of information to assist in setting up this important area:

Traction, by Gino Wickman. This explains the system known as EOS (entrepreneurial operating system). We recommend this book because the concepts expressed in it are valuable and fundamental to any business, no matter the size.

The E Myth Revisited, by Michael Gerber. This book addresses, in clear detail, processes and procedures for creating a smooth-running and profitable business. It also explains how to put together an organizational chart, listing the various positions within the company structure.

Information from these two books will be part of the input we provide as we give you methods to use as you start building your business.

Following are some of the positions we suggest you include on the accountability chart. There may be some that are not included here that you may wish to add. Or there may be some here that will not be required until the business has grown beyond its current size.

At this point, it is likely the same individual's name will come up way too often on this chart. You may also find some positions are not filled, and others may have the wrong person in the role now, but it's a place to start:

BOARD OF DIRECTORS / ADVISORY BOARD

This may consist only of yourself, but this is also a place where many times expertise from others can be of tremendous assistance. This board may include others who are not actually involved in the business but could be a mentor, a coach, or other person who is a valuable resource for you.

CEO / PRESIDENT / MANAGING PARTNER
This likely is you, if you are up to the task. This is the person who administers the decisions of the board of directors. Many times, a very successful company will have as the CEO someone other than the owner. This person must possess many talents and must understand being both the visionary and the implementer. This person must be able to interpret the dream of the visionary but must also be the person who asks the hard questions of how the decisions will be implemented. Most visionaries have a lot of ideas, most of them good, but perhaps not all fit the company. Visionaries also have a very hard problem making their ideas into day-to-day reality.

CFO
The business will be run on your GPS, your business plan, and a lot of that will come down to the budget. Visionaries hate budgets, they serve to stifle their imagination, but the realities of business require that someone sit down, analyze the costs, and analyze the income. Remember, the business is a profit-making enterprise, and profit is not the owner's salary—profit is the return on the investment. Without profit you are growing a nonprofit business, or simply building a job. These can be fine, but what is the goal you have for starting this great enterprise? (Note: this could be a consultant rather than a full-time position.)

GENERAL MANAGER
As the day-to-day manager of the business, this is the person it all rolls down to every single day; this is where the buck stops. The day-to-day operations and the entire business model and its progress depend on him. You must have a person in this position who fully supports the directives of those above him but also must be a person who can effectively communicate with those he reports to and with his staff.

OFFICE MANAGER
Most businesses will have an office, and if there is an office, there needs to be someone in charge.

SALES MANAGER

Will your enterprise need to sell product, a service, or even a combination of these? Someone must manage this segment of the operation.

PRODUCTION / OPERATIONS MANAGER

Will you be producing a product or offering a service? This will require someone to oversee production: track it, measure it, and make the course directions required if the day-to-day production, or process, must be altered.

HUMAN RESOURCES MANAGER

Will your business hire people? If so, this is also a process. And not only that, as you hire people, someone also must manage all the facets of the employment agreement you have. There must be someone responsible for employee benefits and the other factors we do not like to think about in regards the rules and regulations of running a successful business, today and into the future.

SCHEDULING COORDINATOR

Is your product one that will be produced, or is it a service that must be scheduled? Most business models will need someone who is responsible for this scheduling. If you look at the restaurant, hospitality, transportation, or other similar businesses, scheduling is imperative, and if there is a scheduling issue, this will commonly result in monumental problems.

MARKETING DIRECTOR

Marketing and sales are two different things: marketing is bringing prospects to the door to consider a purchase; sales capitalize on marketing to make and close the sale. Marketing is an area where the nature of the customer is changing, and with this, the ability of marketing programs to deliver the right message is key in the success of the business.

ACCOUNTS PAYABLE / ACCOUNTS RECEIVABLE

Your business will have income; this is the receivables. Now, it may be a business that has an instant pay-off: the customer buys and pays for the product at the time of the sale. But there are many businesses that do not have this, and there is an invoicing side. There is also the need for the person in this position to properly credit monies daily on both the expense and the income side. This position is responsible for the collection of the data that the CFO will require to compile the information needed to set the course for the future: to analyze what is happening, to provide the data for the decision-making process of developing new products, and to evaluate the need for the elimination or modification of existing products.

DIRECTOR OF TRAINING
Will your business enterprise require staff members? Will they come with the skills required, or will there need to be a training system constructed to meet the needs of your customer base? In addition, your company must be open to and willing to undergo constant improvement, revising processes to respond to a changing market, or provide a new product. These skills do not materialize overnight.

PRODUCTION PERSONNEL
Will you be making a product? If so, it is likely that you will have personnel who are involved in the production of the product. As such, this is a key role within the business model.

TECHNICIANS
Technicians are the people we send into the field to do installations, maintenance, and to address customer inquiries.

HELPERS/LABORERS
This is more of an unskilled area of the business. It is a position that staff members may start from and then move into the position of a production person or a technician.

FACILITY MANAGER
Who is going to look after the office, change the light bulbs, take out the trash, and clean the bathrooms? These are all needed roles within the business model, and someone must oversee these.

SHIPPING/RECEIVING

Will your business receive products? Will the products be shipped? What are the manpower needs for this area? After all, if we cannot receive or ship the products, how can we do business?

FLEET MAINTENANCE

Will your business have vehicles of some type? If so, someone must maintain them. This could range from doing the maintenance work to contracting out for it to be done.

PURCHASING

Supplies must be bought; they do not simply show up when we need them. This is a role that also must be filled in the enterprise.

WAREHOUSE MANAGER

Will you warehouse or store products? If so, this is a role that requires filling.

It is important that each person understands that he or she is accountable for the requirements of the position to which he or she is assigned.

As you review the various roles in the company, don't consider the person presently doing the job. Rather, you should solely identify the role and who reports to whom. It must also be a rule that a position can only report to one other position. It is common in small business for one person to sit in several seats, which might be the case now. But, the purpose of this suggested chart is to set the organization of the company for future growth.

Creating an accountability structure is one of the most difficult tasks in the process. What you are imagining is the structure of a much larger operation that will more closely resemble the business model you have as a goal.

Initially you may find yourself filling numerous roles, maybe all of them. But your goal as you build the company is determining which roles you like and want to fill and which you want to hand off to someone else as the company grows and matures.

It will also be important to define the roles under each job title with a description of the requirements of the job role. This will be a rather lengthy task, but it is the type of work one must do to work *on* the business, not just *in* the business. Your present business structure presents an owner quite plainly always working in the business but rarely working on the business. Thus, such things as strategic planning, tracking, and monitoring will fall by the wayside.

This has the added benefit of creating a path for others to move into positions of greater responsibility. This is extremely important. When that happens, you will at some point simply serve as a review process to ensure that the results meet your expectations and the goals you have set.

It is likely that you will use outside contractors for some of the positions. One example of that, already mentioned above, is the position of CFO. But many roles can be contracted for, particularly in the early stages, as there is no need for some of them on a full-time basis. You will also need additional outside resources, such as an attorney and tax expert (all areas of tax such as sales, property, income, and corporate).

Once you've created this organizational chart, you can evaluate whether you have the right people to move into these positions. It is crucial you have the right person in the right seat if the business is to grow and meet your goals.

We would suggest that the matter of the organization chart, along with proper job descriptions and expectations, be a top priority for you now. Ultimately, this organization chart will be part of the annual company management review as you set your goals each year.

Remember, you are not just setting up the organization chart for the company as it is today. You are setting this chart up for the company and model you are building. You must form the picture in your mind of the company you want and then make the voyage to get there in the amount of time you allot. Commonly, a growth plan aims at a thirty-six-month target date, with the various segments of the trip broken into smaller, bite-sized goals. One of the things a great manager must do is emulate Mr. Rockefeller and set up his small goals, as defined in the *Traction* book as ROCKs.

12

LEADERSHIP

Leadership skills are not skills any of us are born with: they must be developed. These leadership skills originate with the parenting we received and with the environment we have been reared in and from there, are shaped through the relationships we have developed over the course of our lifetimes. But one thing is certain: the more leadership skills a person has and develops, the further he or she can go in life.

We suggest the book *The 21 Irrefutable Laws of Leadership* be a primary text for anyone who has decided it is time to increase his or her leadership skills. Business owners need leadership as trait for success. No matter the size of the team, you can use the skills of leadership. The skills of leadership extend well beyond the scope of your team; your leadership skills will also be a needed part of your interaction with your customers.

Leadership is an area where you may want to work with a coach, as leadership positions are challenging and can overwhelm you. If you do not work with a coach, then at a minimum find a mentor, a person who can listen to you and who can assist you in finding the answers.

At times, you may even engage the services of a consultant. This is for when things are mounting on you, but it is important to know that a coach and a consultant are two different things. Many coaches and consultants do not understand the difference, but there are dedicated differences that can be easily explained and understood.

CONSULTANT

A contract worker you employ for a short period. Consultants may examine your business and bring you dedicated plans to accomplish a task; they may go further and complete the task for you, or they may simply set the framework in motion. Consultants for specific functions can move you forward rapidly by bringing skills to the table you do not possess.

COACH

The role of the coach is to assist you in formulating the answers. A coach should never be the person who does the specific tasks; rather, the coach works with the person being coached to help him or her building the vision and moving forward to implement on his or her own. Coaches work in all facets of life today, and just like an Olympic athlete will have a coach who sets a medal goal with him or her, the use of a coach by a business leader will enable the leader to move to his or her goals much more rapidly.

Leadership is what builds the next important part of the business model of success. This is a key success factor: this is described as *culture*. One of the ways to look at culture and to understand it was coined by speaker and author Randy Pemberton in answer to a question. When asked to define culture, Randy shared that culture was nothing more than the daily habits of the business, how the business presents itself not only to its customers but also to its prospective customers.

A culture of excellence cannot be built unless the leadership and the members of the team have all bought into the mission. As you build the business of your dreams, remember the long-term success and longevity of your business will depend on the culture you build and grow, along with the manner it is presented to your customers and prospects. After all, you should view satisfied customers as enthused customers; they are who provide our paychecks and our profits.

Always remember, no matter what business you are in, customers are required. Unless you have customers, there is no commerce. We seldom do business with people whom we never interact with in one way or another.

13

FACILITY/WAREHOUSE/PRODUCTION/OFFICE

Will your new enterprise need physical space? This could be for any number of reasons: space for your office, production, warehousing, freight, and even employee parking. Thought processes for the physical location are very important and must be well planned. It is not a pleasant experience when, as your operation comes together, you find out you should relocate or add things that were not properly planned for from the beginning. What looks low cost today could turn out to be a very costly decision at a later point. Location, zoning, access, and so many other things will come into play in the decision-making process. Your business plan must include what you will do as you expand and grow, and when you anticipate that this facility will no longer work for you.

14

EQUIPMENT/TOOLING

What tooling and equipment will be required for you to make, produce, or supply your product? Under this we also have the question of vehicles: Will there be vehicles required by your business to deliver or install your product? Perhaps they will be used by the sales force as well. Take a hard look at your needs and then anticipate and project, and of course each of these decisions goes back to the funding question. It all must be paid for.

15

COMPANY SIZE–WHAT IS YOUR GOAL?

This is one you need to be looking at from the start and one that often catches people by surprise at a later point. The right answer is a size that satisfies your needs—as the owner—but also the size the market will support.

A prospective business owner, as a part of the plan, needs to decide just how big the business will become. In addition to satisfying the owner's and the market's needs, the size of the business will depend on your comfort zone. Perhaps your business may employ hundreds, even thousands. Or it could be a few people—perhaps just you.

The one thing you as the prospective business owner do not want to do is build a business that is not what you want, one that provides nothing but chaos. You need to make this decision. A common question we would ask you in a face-to-face discussion is the following:

Close your eyes, and paint a picture in words. What do you see your business as being in three years, five years, and ten years? What does this picture show? Once you know that and you know the market can support it, then you can build the business through a series of short-terms goals to reach what is truly your long-term goal.

16

PRICING/MARGINS

You must develop the pricing for the product. The pricing must be determined with purpose; the product will deliver value to the customer at the price being set. But equally important is that the pricing must be such that you, the owner of the business, can draw the income needed to cover the expenses of the business and deliver a return on your investment.

Price is generally shaped by market forces, meaning there is a maximum that the market is willing to pay for your product. This is based on your competitors' pricing, your value proposition, and your position in your marketplace. As you contemplate your pricing, not only do you need to understand where your pricing fits within these three parameters, but you also need to be cognizant of your costs. You will need to have a good handle on the cost of your product, along with the overhead cost of running your company. The support functions that you will need to provide—customer service, bookkeeping, warehousing, delivery vehicles, and so forth—are key components to servicing your customer. Your pricing will need to support those critical functions. As an owner, you also need to draw a salary and build equity in your company. These last two areas are paramount, for if you fail to achieve them, you are only providing jobs to others and will have nothing left at the end of the day for yourself.

Therefore, it is very worthwhile to invest your time in this area of business planning—you will reap the rewards of your efforts as your business grows.

17

WHAT IS YOUR SALES STRATEGY?

How will the product be taken to market, what is your sales strategy, and what are the sales channels it will be delivered through? Will your product go directly from you to the end user, or will there be steps in between? It is important to note that each step will require points, a term used to describe the percentage of the price each intermediate step will take from the selling price of the product. Too many steps can often result in the business operating in the red, making plenty of products but losing money with each piece sold and delivered.

A part of your business plan should be the formulation of your sales strategy. This will become the sales map that delivers sales in the proper manner to provide for sustainability of the business. The sales strategy must be designed to match with the capability of the company to produce the product.

18

OPERATING SYSTEMS / SOFTWARE

Is there a need for computer systems to be used? Currently bookkeeping is usually a computer system using off-the-shelf software. What about the business you are putting together? Will it require computers and software to function properly and effectively? Operating systems and software should always have benefits and should never be a drag on the company profits or efficiency. Good systems and software make you money—they do not cost you money. The smart manager always looks at the best value but also views it from the viewpoint of return on the investment, not just on cost!

19

STANDARD OPERATING SYSTEMS / PROCEDURES (SOPs)

It is assumed you have done your homework by reviewing *The E Myth Revisited*, one of the books suggested earlier. This section is designed to assist you in the process of developing standard operating procedures, or SOPs.

Until a company develops and adopts SOPs, each person in the company is left to create his or her own way of doing things. And we end up with numerous and often inefficient ways to accomplish a task.

This makes the training of new employees problematic. As you add new employees, they develop the habits of the person who trained them, along with their whims and desires of how to do the job. This may not deliver the desired results.

SOPs are created to eradicate waste, increase productivity, and ensure all are working on the same path to the same goal. It will only work, however, if all members of the company follow these procedures, including management.

You must start the process of asking three questions each time an issue arises. They are as follows:

- Is there no SOP to cover this?
- Was the SOP complied with?
- Was the SOP wrong?

Once these questions are asked and you have a direction, you will find that the development of SOPs as operating guidelines, although an ongoing process, becomes easier and easier. But again, this is a part of working on the business that must be done.

One thing that must also be understood is that creating SOPs is not just done by the CEO or general manager. There must be involvement from your team of experts, the folks that work for you. This is one of those tasks that must be addressed now. It will prove to be one of the best ways to equip your team members for the task ahead. Because of this, we suggest the following course of action to get the program up and running:

DETERMINE FOR WHICH TASKS SOPS ARE NEEDED
Assign the draft of the SOP to your expert on this subject. Make sure he or she understands you are only looking for simple, clear, overall guidelines. Have the draft reviewed by the GM, department head, or person best equipped to do so. It should be the person responsible for supervising those charged with completing the specified task. Review by management: Does this meet your approval?

HAND SOP OFF TO STAFF MEMBERS FOR REVIEW
They have two or three days max to review and come back with suggestions. If they fail to get back to you in that time, consider the SOP approved.

GIVE THE NEW SOP TO SOMEONE WHO HAS NEVER DONE THE TASK
Can that person now do it by following the SOP? Remember, one of our goals is to hand this to a new hire and say, "Do it," and he or she can do it simply from following the procedure as written.

IMPLEMENTATION
Each SOP must be dated. You may be amending it later. Dates of amendment or modification must be noted.

ANNUAL REVIEW OF THE SOP

This needs to be done to ensure it still is current and still works.

SOP MODIFICATION

SOPs must be modified as required if they prove to be ineffectual or impractical. All staff members should be advising you when an SOP presents issues or when an SOP is needed where there is not one now. That means everyone must be included in this process of constant review.

The SOPs should be accessible electronically and in a printed form by all employees. This will be an ongoing part of the company protocol.

We ask each client to set a goal as to how many SOPs they will produce in a month and how many in total are needed to ensure the business can operate in a way that no one must ask anyone else how any task is done. By doing that, you are also building value in the company and taking work off your shoulders.

20

WHAT IS YOUR MARKETING STRATEGY?

Product and services do not just move on their own, and in today's world, the marketing of a business has gotten more and more complicated. And the rules will change depending on your location, your reach (are you selling locally, regionally, or on a national level), and whether you are selling to end consumers or to businesses. Without a background in marketing, this is an area where one is commonly advised to consult with outside sources or even contract for expert services. The following are offered as examples of marketing ideas for consideration:

WEBSITE
No business in today's age and time can properly present themselves without a well-written and -presented website. The website of today, along with the various search engines, will crawl the Internet, read you website, and work to promote what you do to your prospects. Your website needs to be designed to be picked up by the various search engines and promote what you do for your prospective customers.

SOCIAL MARKETING
Social media is largely underused by many businesses today. It can encompass many different media, and the list is long. Here are just a few examples:

Facebook
Instagram
Twitter
LinkedIn

Snapchat
YouTube
Pinterest

And the list goes on. The key to social networks is that you should be socially active where your prospects dwell. And dwell they do. However, social media is not for promotions as a rule; it is more for building authority and to show value to prospects. This is an important part of any marketing strategy; your prospect is looking for value, and it is through these media that you project this value.

Social media engagement requires time, and companies that cannot afford to spend the time will commonly contract out to others to present an effective social presence.

VIDEOS
In today's world, videos are a premier marketing method. The number-one medium for videos is not television—it is access through various Internet offerings. YouTube has become a tremendous content-delivery vehicle and one that many are effectively using to promote products and services.

NETWORKING
Networking is a phenomenal way to market products and services. This is done via many different formats; it can be through associations, civic organizations, churches, and many other similar groups. Your local chamber of commerce will expose you to others. Network marketing exposes you to prospects, but it also has the potential of building up your referral marketing, of which networking is a big part. Many communities have local BNI (Business Networking International) groups, and many find that if the right group is located, this can be a gold mine of business.

PRINTED PROMOTIONAL PIECES
Many times, a business will need to invest in printed materials to promote its products and itself. The printing must be done in a quality manner to portray you and your company as being value propositions. Value is not about the lowest cost; rather, it is

about how the product provides and, if possible, exceeds the value the prospective customer is looking for.

REPEAT BUSINESS MARKETING
Most businesses benefit from the value of repeat business, as there is less cost to maintain a business relationship than there is to build one. A part of your marketing strategy is how you will retain the customer base you are busting your tail to gain.

REFERRAL / TESTIMONIALS MARKETING
It is often viewed that testimonial-driven sales are the easiest to make. A part of your marketing strategy should include how to garner your reviews and testimonials. To quote a noted sales coach, author, and speaker Jeffrey Gitomer, there is only one way to gain these: you earn them. As you put your plan together, include in it how you are going to gain the testimonial-driven sales that your customer base will offer you.

DIRECT MAIL
Direct mail can be an effective means of gaining market share, but your direct mail must be pointed to who your customer is. It is just like fishing: you don't want to be casting your line into waters that do not contain fish; this is the same for the direct-mail marketing concept.

MARKETING TRACKING AND MEASUREMENT PROCESSES
An important part of the business marketing plan must include a deep analysis of the data to determine if your marketing dollars are delivering. Each business owner must know the cost of procurement of the customer: What did it cost to make the telephone ring, and what did it cost to get the customer to place the initial order (and any following orders)? A system of data collection is of utmost importance to this.

21

STAFF RECRUITMENT / HUMAN RESOURCES

RECRUITMENT AND SELECTION

Taking a professional approach to recruitment and developing procedures to support this approach will enable your organization to find the best candidates for your jobs, even considering changing times. An active recruiting program is the primary and best solution to ensuring adequate staffing.

As the previous chapter highlighted, there are certain steps that must be taken regarding employment. Consideration should be given to the current makeup of your workforce. Relying solely on referrals from the current workforce may result in underrepresentation of certain protected groups. It is important that the community at large be made and kept aware of your present and future needs. One way to do this is to develop and maintain relationships with local colleges, universities, technical schools, minority and women's group leaders, churches, and so forth, which may refer qualified candidates to your organization. Relationships with recruiting sources prove most beneficial when you take the time and effort to help them understand your need for top-quality applicants.

One government agency that must be notified of job openings is your state employment agency. The Vietnam Era Veterans Readjustment Act of 1974 requires that all full-time positions be listed with these agencies. This is especially crucial if you are a federal contractor.

DOS AND DON'TS

Do: Employers have the right to decide whether an applicant has the requisite skills or work experience to perform a particular task. Therefore, it is highly recommended that reference checks be conducted. While it is a fact that in to-day's climate you may not get much useful information from a previous employer, making the effort to obtain the information may insulate the organization from a future negligent hiring claim.

Don't: An employer cannot impose a requirement of a certain level of education simply to improve the overall quality of the workforce. To prevent this type of discrimination, an employer may only require a certain level of education when it directly relates to the requirements of the job.

Do: An employer can lawfully refuse to hire an applicant who has been convicted of certain classes of felonies. Under the law, it must be demonstrated that there is a relationship between the conviction and the specific job. It is highly recommended that all candidates for employment be subjected to a thorough criminal background check, both at the state and federal level. This is especially crucial given the limited reference information we may be able to obtain, as mentioned previously.

Don't: An employer may not automatically disqualify an applicant based on a criminal conviction. Consideration must be given based on the type of crime, the number of years since the conviction, and specific job requirements.

RECRUITING SOURCES

Today there seems to be a never-ending list of Internet-based recruiting options. For many positions, the web can be the most cost-effective way to reach interested candidates. The social media explosion is a prime example of this. Essentially, though, social media recruiting harkens back to the age-old recruiting mantra of "network, network, network."

Many of the sources below can be used in cooperation with web solutions. Ultimately, there is no definitive list of top recruiting options for any one business. As a manager, it is up to you to know the specific needs of your organization and determine the best recruiting sources to fit your needs.

COLLEGES, UNIVERSITIES, AND OTHER SCHOOLS

Educational institutions are great sources for entry-level candidates. Many organizations forget, though, that college students make great part-time employees, as many of them must work to pay for school. A relationship can be developed with the placement office, ads placed in the college newspaper, and posters hung in areas where the students congregate to recruit potential employees.

DISCHARGED MILITARY PERSONNEL

Recruiting recently discharged military personnel can be extremely beneficial to a business. Many veterans gain valuable skills in the military that are easily transferrable to civilian work. It is important to develop relationships with officers who counsel departing service personnel.

FRIENDS/RELATIVES OF CURRENT EMPLOYEES

Current employees with good track records may be an excellent recruiting source for you. The key here is to inform your workforce of current openings and the skills you require for those positions.

JOB FAIRS

The challenge with job fairs is that you can never be sure about the type of individuals who will attend the event, and some events can be pricey. Prior to investing in a job fair, attempt to verify with the organizer the type of individual they expect to attract, the numbers of attendees at previous events, and the satisfaction level of other employers that have attended the event.

HEADHUNTERS

While certainly not a good option for all positions, for hard-to-recruit positions outsourcing may be the best option. Headhunters charge a fee based on a successful placement. Fees usually start around 25 percent of the candidate's annual salary. If using a headhunter, it is advisable to obtain a service guarantee. This involves a commitment from the headhunter to refund a portion of the placement fee if the candidate terminates employment within a specified period.

TEMPORARY HELP AGENCIES

Temporary, or temp, help is an excellent way to staff a growing operation. It offers flexibility and perhaps more importantly, the opportunity to take a "trial run" with a prospective employee. While the hourly fee charged by a staffing agency is higher than what you might pay an employee, remember that they are conducting all the background checks and providing all benefits to the individual.

CO-OPS AND INTERNS

As mentioned previously in the "Colleges, universities, and other schools" section, providing college students with on-the-job learning opportunities may be a win-win situation. The organization can fill a need, and the student gains valuable experience. Typically, the intern does not earn what a fully qualified employee would, and, as with temporary employees, the organization gets a "test run" on the person.

ADVERTISING

While nothing can replace the one-on-one contacts we have previously discussed, on occasion we may have no recourse except to advertise for our openings. In today's environment, if you decide to advertise, the web is the place to be. There are literally thousands of job boards out there, many of which are geared toward specific jobs, industries, and even types of candidates.

Planning for your recruitment needs enables you to develop the necessary relationships, contacts, and sources and to anticipate costs. It is highly advisable to track the effectiveness of each recruiting source. This includes cost, number of applications received, interviews conducted, candidates hired, and first year turnover. Remember, the goal of recruiting is not to generate lots of applicants; it is to hire a fully qualified and ultimately successful employee. Tracking statistics over the long term will guide your organization in making future recruiting decisions.

22

STAFF TRAINING

There is no doubt about it: employee training can be quite expensive, particularly for small businesses.

EMPLOYEE CROSS-TRAINING

It's a situation small-business owners know all too well: unforeseen or extended employee absences can impact business productivity. The solution is to cross-train your employees. For example, when you are bringing on a new hire, make sure your current employees treat him or her with a friendly and helpful attitude and are patient while being asked questions during the first few weeks. For even greater impact, pair up new and veteran employees to tackle new challenges. This plan is simple. By sharing their techniques and knowledge, employees show their fellow colleagues how to perform their most significant tasks, so their responsibilities are fulfilled during work absences. This cross-training allows you to develop a workforce that is prepared for long-term absences and is more knowledgeable of your business's operations.

Before you embark on a training program, be specific about what you and your employees want to achieve. Use annual performance reviews to gauge competency gaps as well as your employees' desired areas of improvement. Then put specific training goals in place for each employee. Let your employees know that you will assess the impact the training has had on their overall job skills and performance on a six-month and annual basis.

BROWN-BAG SEMINARS

A more informal method of employee training is using brown-bag seminars, offered during your employees' lunch breaks. These sessions are best kept voluntary and, for the most part, casual and free. If you make attendance at these sessions mandatory, you will have to pay your employees for the training. Always consult a professional knowledgeable in the employment laws in your industry and state for guidance.

- Brown-bag seminars allow employees to interact with one another on a wide range of training topics, making these interactions increase employee bonds and, ultimately, improve teamwork.
- Most brown-bag sessions should be an hour long or less, to avoid taking too much time away from employees' busy schedules.
- Give all your employees the opportunity to facilitate a session. The result is a more confident team, as they can practice their leadership and communication skills.

DON'T DO IT ALL YOURSELF!

Bring in experts to teach skills or help you and your employees gain knowledge in new areas. Or send employees to training programs or schools for advanced training. Contact industry organizations and peruse trade journals for information on certifications or training schools within your industry. Your local chamber of commerce as well as contacts in your business network can often provide recommendations for general business skills such as marketing, finance, and productivity.

IMMERSION TRAINING

Some skills, such as communication, problem solving, collaboration, and technology use, can benefit everyone in the business, regardless of job role. To train your whole staff or an entire department, set aside a day or more for immersion training. Close the shop (or do the training after hours) so that everyone can spend consecutive hours learning about and practicing the new skill. This type of immersion training benefits new and experienced employees alike.

Both your business and your employees will benefit from simplified, strategic training. And don't forget about improving and expanding your own skills! The more equipped you are as a business owner, the better you can train and equip your employees.

FINALLY, CONSIDER ONLINE TRAINING

This can be an affordable way to get employees trained and can be done from anywhere, at any time. Numerous providers offer well-priced options that are suitable across any industry. For industry specific training, many local chambers of commerce and trade associations have options.

In a nutshell: employees' attitudes are reflected in their behaviors. These attitudes come from their feelings about the work environment and those around them. Training programs should *not* concentrate on fixing attitudes but on creating a willingness to perform and behave appropriately. Ultimately, employees change their behavior due to training. Remember, your workplace climate determines the level of success your training program achieves.

23

STAFF COMPENSATION AND BENEFITS

A well-defined compensation program provides rewards for meeting and exceeding employee performance expectations. To be effective, such a program must be individualized, while providing for internal equity among jobs and maintaining parity with market rates. The process requires accurate and current job descriptions, an effective evaluation system, consistently applied administrative policies, and open communication between management and employees.

- Establish compensation program philosophy and objectives
- Identify job classifications and define them—revise job descriptions as needed
- Determine compensable factors for each classification
- Evaluate each job relative to other jobs and place them in the appropriate job classification
- Consult current salary surveys to establish market rates for each job classification, based on benchmark jobs
- Establish pay grades for each job classification to reflect the company's appropriate position within the labor market
- Establish a plan to implement any necessary compensation adjustments, in line with budgetary considerations
- Develop administrative procedures to reflect new policies, rates, and management responsibilities for maintaining the program
- Communicate the compensation program to management and employees
- Design and implement performance management systems to complement compensation processes and tie performance to compensation
- Train management team on effective performance appraisal techniques

24

TRACKING AND MEASUREMENT

As the budget is developed, tracking must also be developed to include both income and expenses. This sets you up with the ability to analyze the cost of individual jobs. Through this method, you can determine your cost of doing business and decide what to charge, after which you can set a course to deliver the return you want to achieve. This allows you to formulate your sales goal, which is also a part of the tracking system that will require development. As part of this, you will need to track the performance/efficiency/effectiveness of each tech.

All in all, this tracking protocol will alert you as to how to build on the strengths and to work to eliminate the weaknesses that prevent you from reaching your sales goals. Here are a couple of questions you should ask yourself:

- How much does a lead cost you?
- What is the average sale per customer?
- What is the net profit on a sale?
- What is the net profit on an installation?
- What percentage of your annual gross is spent on labor?
- What is the percentage of work you get from each possible source: word of mouth, website, social marketing, referral from other companies, Angie's List, and so forth?
- What quantity did you sell in (*time period*)?
- What was the average cost?
- What is the sales goal in (*time period*)?

These are just examples of the types of questions that you will answer from tracking and measurement. From this, you can build a system of cash flow forecasting to ensure you are meeting or exceeding your goals and, if needed, take corrective action. This is the information you need to obtain from the data in order to "up your game."

But the tracking also enables you to determine what your waste is and how to cut it. This is a serious issue with many companies, but it is not seen because it is hidden beneath the surface activity of working *in* business day to day rather than *on* it. And so, the waste pile continues to grow.

Consider the following for a minute: 95 percent of the average waste in a company comes from labor (man hours), and 5 percent comes from materials. If you can cut waste by 5 percent, you can usually raise the company profit by 35 percent.

Let's dig a little deeper. The average worker wastes about $275 per day. Multiply that by your number of workers, and the figure really becomes alarming. For instance, if we say we have seven workers (two part-time, and six full-time) and if our daily waste is $275 per day, that means our waste per day for the company is $1925. Let's go a little further. In a five-day workweek, that will be an average week at $9,625. To make it just a little scarier, let's figure on an average year of forty-eight weeks, and this reveals an average waste per year of $462,000. Or you could look at the average number of chargeable days in a year, typically around 180, and you would come up with a figure of "only" $345,500 of waste annually.

25

LEAN PROCESSES

"Lean" refers to the process of removing the excess baggage, outdated processes, and duplication of effort from every aspect of a company's operation. It is an ongoing process that becomes part of the company culture. Many of the suggestions we have offered in this document such as regular meetings, SOPs, strategic hiring processes, formalized training, and so forth, are part of a lean culture in a company. It is all included in what it takes to accomplish more with less by conserving resources. It results in reducing the occurrence of injuries, wasted time, wasted effort, and sloppy operational procedures that distract management from the more important issues facing the company. In short, it gets rid of waste.

26

MEETINGS

It is very important to structure regular, substantive meetings with company personnel. No meeting should ever be held simply to have a meeting. A meeting should never be held without deciding who will run the meeting and what the specific agenda will be. Straying from this procedure runs the risk of making the meeting ineffective and counterproductive. The meeting process is one that, if started from the beginning and then expanded as the company grows, enables you to track the daily results of the company and to conceive and implement results quickly.

We suggest you schedule the following meetings:

DAILY POWER MEETING

This meeting is done every morning at a set time, no matter what. Ideally this should be held in the same location daily. No one is seated for this meeting. It should be conducted by someone who can do this without emotion; this is not a blame-game time, this is a process.

The purpose of this meeting is to review the prior day. Were we productive? Were we profitable? Did we meet our delivery objectives? Did we meet our quality standards? Did we meet our add-on sales goals? Did we complete the day safely? The objectives for each of those considerations can be whatever you determine. But there should only be these six areas addressed initially, and any variation from your acceptable outcomes for these areas should be noted and recorded.

In this meeting, we are reporting to the team how we did yesterday, but we are also extracting data to use in the managers meeting later.

The morning power meeting should last five to seven minutes max. It is critical that this be a reporting meeting, not a meeting for rebuttals, explanations, objections, or to cast blame. The data extracted is important for furthering the management of the company.

The daily morning meeting should be observed by all company managers, including the production manager, to assure that the meeting is fulfilling its purpose. One of the most difficult tasks many owners face is to properly administer this meeting. It must be controlled, it must be unemotional, it must drill down on each issue, and no one should ever have to defend him- or herself in this meeting.

One of the hardest concepts for leaders to understand is that if anything goes wrong under their ownership or management, the fault is theirs. They let it happen. If we have an unproductive, untrained, or uncooperative team member, we must understand that it is our fault. This understanding is a crucial part of successful management.

MANAGERS MEETING

This meeting is done on a weekly basis. In this meeting, we review the past week and we use the data we have extracted in the daily meetings to formulate strategies for how we will move forward. This is where we identify any SOP needs, approve new or revised SOPs, and assign tasks. This meeting should be conducted with the general manager and the department managers.

Key department managers to be included are office and production managers. This meeting should take less than one hour and should always conclude with items to be completed, the person assigned each task, and a timeline for completion. As with the daily power meetings, it is essential that this meeting follows a set agenda.

WEEKLY COMPANY MEETING

This is for all employees. It is the meeting to go over the success and the failures of the prior week, announce new programs, introduce new SOPs, and make the team feel and function as a cohesive group. The purpose of this meeting is to align the goals of management and staff. All managers must be involved. Managers must take notes and be prepared to use any pertinent information or data discussed during the meeting.

SEMIANNUAL COMPANY MEETING

In this meeting, we deliver the long-term report card, which includes how we have done as a company and what the coming months present as far as changes in the company, challenges, new strategies, and new markets. The semiannual meeting continues to move your team forward as a cohesive unit because it includes them in planning, goal setting, and strategies.

This will assure buy-in from all team members. I suggest this meeting be conducted prior to the seasonal market changes the business may undergo. These will be the times of greatest change in the market and the way we do business.

ANNUAL MEETING

This is a time to celebrate your accomplishments and review your progress as a company. It is also when you present the company's goals for the future. Again, it serves the purpose of making everyone feel included in successes, failures, goals, plans, and strategies. That's how they come to feel like they are part of a team rather than just employees.

SAME-PAGE MEETING

There is a need for a meeting of the partners of the business, if there are any. The purpose will be to make sure owners are on the same page as far as the present position and direction of the company. This makes certain the visionary and the integrator are aligned, all is well, and everything is on track.

What leaders must understand and remember is that although this sounds like a regimented system for meetings that seems unwieldy and takes up time, once instituted, it is a way to increase efficiency, lift morale, and save time. This is a dedicated part of the lean plan of business operations. However, again, each meeting must have an agenda and a purpose. If this is done, then the value is immense.

27

GOALS

It is critical that you assemble both short- and long-term goals. Short-term goals are created to provide the road map for obtaining the long-term goals. This is done in a systematic manner so the long-term goals can be attained on schedule. We stress the importance of setting these on a thirty-day and a ninety-day format.

28

EXIT PLAN / INCLUDING TIME FRAME FOR PLANNED EXIT

First, what is an exit plan? Your exit plan should be what you want to do with the business when you are ready to move on. The best part: there is no wrong answer to this question! It's all up to you. And you don't have to have a firm answer on the day you start your business; the answer can evolve over time. It is, however, important that you have a plan.

As you consider what your exit looks like—no longer involved in day-to-day operations, owner from a remote location, serial entrepreneur, on to the next challenge—you will start to formulate a strategy and a plan. This strategy will begin to guide your longer-term planning and decision-making activities (e.g., annual budget, investing and acquisition activities, etc.). The ultimate goal is to maximize your outcome—both in terms of plan achievement and monetary return.

Is the business owner-centric, or can it run without you? This is a major issue for small-business owners who are looking to sell. Training and a good succession plan for employees (especially in a general manager role) may be the difference between a maximized valuation and a paltry one.

To maximize your monetary return, your exit should be timed to be at a point where your business is achieving outstanding financial results. You may have heard the adage "buy low, sell high"—this can be true for selling a business as well. Buyers will be looking at the last three to five years of operating/financial performance to place a value on the business. If you aren't selling in this position of strength (from the seller's perspective), you may be forced into a price that values only the customer list that you bring to the table. This is far less valuable than a vibrant business that owns its market, delivers value to its customers, and consistently provides a strong ROI to the investor/owner.

A buyer can also come from within your company—selling to family members or key managers can provide more continuity and stability compared to selling to a buyer with means but no experience. A sales transaction to internal parties may be more flexible to negotiate in terms of timing, price, and other key provisions. You may be able to negotiate a transition plan that includes staying on in a paid consultative role for a period, while key personnel are trained in their roles. This also allows for the buy-out to occur over time, such that the buyer(s) would not have a need to take on debt to complete the purchase. There are many creative ways to complete a transaction; whichever you decide, make sure the legal documents are in place that formalize the understanding of all parties to the transaction.

29

GO TIME!

There's no time like the present to start working on building the business of your dreams. We've provided a wealth of hands-on, "been there, done that" information to get you out of the starting blocks and into the race. All you've got to do is (1) believe in yourself, (2) find your motivation, and (3) stay the course. Two of these are all *you*! The third is covered in the content of this book.

There will be many things that you will learn on your journey, just as we have. We want to share our experiences with you through this book—the joys, the pains, the trials, the triumphs—all included here, so you can avoid some of the pitfalls that await entrepreneurs on the path to building that dream of owning your own business.

One of the biggest challenges you will face is hiring the right people. You've probably heard the phrase "People are your most important asset." While this is true, they will also be your most expensive asset. Take your time, and hire the right people. Provide them the tools and training to succeed. Train them, and develop them. But most of all, treat them fairly. Good employees are worth their weight in gold. They will run through walls for you. Bad employees will cause you headaches and perhaps cost you customers. There is only one way to know what will motivate your employees to do good work for you: ask them! Find out how they want to be rewarded. While not everyone is motivated by money, they may not want another mug with the company logo on it either! Take the time to truly get to know what makes your people tick. It will make you a better owner, and they will feel valued. That's a win-win in anyone's book.

Planning is often forgotten once the business plan has been presented to a bank or other funding source. Think of business planning as the GPS for your business—the path to your ultimate destination. Whether it is financial, strategic, operational, or organizational, your plans are a way to get your thoughts and ideas about your business on paper, ready to share with your advisors and employees for feedback and implementation. Moreover, planning is a great way to test out your ideas *before* you spend money on them and potentially make some big mistakes. It's always best to know the result of a decision on paper before you make major financial commitments. This is true in the hiring process; hiring the right people takes planning—a job description, cohesive organizational structure, compensation and benefits research, and top-notch recruiting. It's no different when you plan the financials for your business; you need to plan for more cash coming into your business than leaving your business for long-term viability and ultimate success.

It is the American Dream of so many to build a business—some call it entrepreneurship, but others simply look at it as their dream. Some may desire to take this path because they feel that they want to forge their own course in life, or perhaps they just want to go a place that working for others does not allow. But the sad fact is that too many fail to achieve this dream. It can wreck one's life savings, and it can also compromise one's work-life balance. As a coach, I have worked with many for whom the business just never produces the dreams they envisioned for any number of reasons. But overall, business failure can usually boil down to what we know and how we apply our knowledge. Many can overcome the technical hurdles, but the management and administration of the business often boggles the mind. Building a business is hard work, usually much harder than many entrepreneurs ever realized. And often the clients I work with have twenty or more years in the business, and they finally say to a coach or consultant, "I need help!" Often it is due to the feeling of being overwhelmed by all the different things one must know and execute to be a success.

Our purpose in writing this book as a team was to share with you, the reader, the various parts of the business that must mesh and how they work together for the success we envision for your business. This book is intended to give readers a well-rounded view of how to guide their business to the destination they truly want. While not making you an expert, the various areas we have covered do present a well-rounded view of what the elements of the foundation for a successful business looks like. We hope that this is a value to you, the reader.

If this book enables you to gain the insight to reach your dreams as you build and perfect your business, then our goal has been fulfilled.

THE AUTHORS

Jerry Isenhour is a business coach, strategist, and educator based in Charlotte, North Carolina, who specializes in blue-collar home service contracting businesses. In his coaching and consulting practice, he works in all areas of the country. His résumé also includes experience as the CEO of companies in service, retail, and manufacturing. Also, he has served as the president of national trade groups and education foundations and on industry certification governing boards.

Jerry is a certified member of the John Maxwell Team as a leadership coach, teacher, and speaker. He is also a certified sales adviser with certification by Jeffrey Gitomer. He presently serves as the CEO and lead coach at CVC Coaching, a full-service coaching, educational provider, and consulting organization providing expertise to clients across the United States.

Jerry developed his thirst for the processes of SOPs and SOGs (Standard Operating Guidelines) in his own service business after reading books and studies on how the military and successful business managers ran their businesses according to a strict system that controlled all operations. A part of this was his review of *The E Myth,* by Michael Gerber, and hearing the author speak. He quickly saw the value of the SOP process, and he began building SOPs/SOGs for his businesses, which included a chimney service company, a retail venture that sold specialty products for the outdoor living and fireplace industry, and a manufacturing company producing a product for the outdoor living industry.

During his time as the owner of various business endeavors, he also was highly involved in trade and educational groups on the state, regional, and national levels and has presented educational offerings to the industries he serves since 1984. Having trained thousands of business owners and technicians, he has become known as an expert in his fields.

In 2010, he became a coach and consultant to the industries in which he carried expertise, and today he works across the United States in his capacity as a teacher, coach, consultant, and educator. Even though he works with a wide variety of subject matters from both the technical and the operational side of the business, his true expertise as a systems expert has been one of his success foundations.

The first book authored by Jerry was titled *Chaos to Reinvention* and is the story of how the chaos disrupted his life and inspired him to become a coach for blue-collar business owners and managers. He is also a coauthor of the book *The Daily Difference Life Lessons,* available on Amazon and other book sellers. And his most recent release was *Standardizing Standard Operating Procedures,* which provides a comprehensive eight-step process for the composition and communication of SOPs and SOGs that work.

Jerry has also authored numerous items that have included journal articles and is considered as a source of expertise on the subject matters he writes about and his coaching practice covers. He also prepares seminars, keynotes, and talks on these subjects, and his audience is spread across the United States. His words, advice, counsel, and perspective are considered invaluable assets by many business owners.

To find out more about Jerry, visit his websites:

www.cvccoaching.com
www.jerryisenhour.com

Facebook: CVC Coaching
YouTube: CVCCoaching
Twitter: JerryCVC
Instagram: CVCJerry
LinkedIn: Jerry Isenhour

Also tune in to his podcast *The Chimney & Fireplace Success Network* on Soundcloud, Stitcher, and iTunes.

Feel free to contact Jerry. You can contact him through e-mail at jerry@cvccoaching.com. He will be glad to schedule a call with you to help you in your pursuit of the production of a library of SOPs and SOGs for your business.

Ed Krow, SPHR, CCP, SHRM-SCP, of TurboExecs, partners with results-oriented businesses that are struggling with people problems that are having a negative impact on the business, such as adapting to changing business conditions and customer/investor/community expectations.

He helps them put in place HR best practices, learning and development plans, and toal reward systems so they employee incentivize performance in alignment with their business goals. Ed's clients often refer to him as their "safety net," because he keeps them from falling into HR traps and eliminates HR headaches.

When he's not working with clients, Ed can be found teaching at Millersville University or speaking at human resources conferences, seminars, and professional development sessions. In his free time, Ed enjoys family time, travel, golf, the outdoors and Notre Dame and Baltimore Ravens football.

To learn more about Ed, visit:
www.TurboExecs.com
Facebook: TurboExecs
YouTube: TurboExecs
Twitter: @TurboExecs, @EdKrowHR
LinkedIn: Ed Krow

You can contact Ed directly via e-mail at ed@TurboExecs.com.

As a partner at TurboExecs, Patty Lawrence, CMA, works with results-oriented small- and medium-business owners who are struggling with chaos, such as out-of-control growth, sudden terrifying decline in revenues or profits, or people problems that are having a negative impact on the business.

She reveals the "story behind the numbers" with financial tools and systems that quickly skyrocket productivity and remove barriers to growth and profitability. As a result, her clients typically increase the bottom line by at least 15 percent and feel in control of their finances and results.

Patty got her first taste of entrepreneurial life in the office of her father's well-drilling business in her teens. With her first accounting class in high school, she'd found the professional outlet for her problem-solving skills.

Patty is a graduate of Indiana University in Bloomington, Indiana, where she received her bachelor of science degree in accounting with a concentration in French. She earned her certified management accountant (CMA) designation in 1991 and is a member of the Institute of Management Accountants. She is a graduate of Leadership Lancaster, served on the board of the Hempfield Soccer Club, the Finance/Audit/Compliance Committee for St. Joseph Health Ministries, the Finance Committee at her church, and is past board chair of the Hempfield Area Recreation Commission.

She is a frequent speaker on accounting topics at conferences and teaches accounting and finance to entrepreneurs at Penn State Harrisburg. In her free time, Patty enjoys playing competitive tennis, cooking, and travel.

To learn more about Patty, visit:
www.TurboExecs.com
Facebook: TurboExecs
YouTube: TurboExecs
Twitter: @TurboExecs, @_PattyLawrence
LinkedIn: Patty Lawrence

You can contact Patty directly via e-mail at patty@TurboExecs.com. You have a grand vision for your business, but you can't DIY everything and expect to get there. With more management horsepower, however, you *can* achieve the business of your dreams. Call Patty at 717.925.3270 if you think it might be time to add the horsepower of a CFO to your business. Then we can schedule your free Turbocharge Your Business session.

Made in the USA
Columbia, SC
30 November 2020

25763120R00043